'Eight of the newest Head-dresses of 1777'. These tall hairstyles were achieved by combing natural hair and false hair together over pads of wool and horsehair and greasing with a liberal quantity of pomatum.

WIGS AND WIGMAKING

In 1624 Louis XIII of France went prematurely bald. He disguised this with a wig and started a fashion that lasted for over one hundred and fifty years. Wigs arrived in England in 1660 when Royalists returned from exile in France after the restoration of Charles II.

Early wigs were little more than cloth skull caps with tufts of hair stitched on. Later the foundation was animal skin and subsequently a net base was used. The seventeenth-century full-bottomed wig was large and flamboyant with cascades of brown or black curls falling to below the shoulders. They were expensive and could cost from £3 to £20.

The full-bottomed wig was out of fashion by about 1720 although it continued to be worn by old men and professionals for a further twenty years. It was replaced by a wider variety of styles that were generally shorter and more artificial in appearance, with names like the Brutus and the Cauliflower.

The bob, a style that stopped below the ears, was first worn in the 1680s by tradesmen who could not afford the larger style. Gradually it became widely acceptable socially and became the standard wear for eighteenth-century clergy. The tie-wig had the hair combed back into a tail fixed with a ribbon at the nape of the neck. When the tail was secured in a black silk pouch it was known as a bag wig and this style was popular with the gentry from about 1725. Styles became very exaggerated in the 1770s and the macaronis or young men of fashion wore enormous wigs dressed over pads of greased wool and horsehair.

Women never adopted wigs with the same enthusiasm as men and in the

Sir Cloudesley Shovell (1650-1707), Admiral of the Fleet, in a heavy full-bottomed wig with a mass of tight curls framing the face. The wig named after him was brown with six or eight clusters of curls hanging low. Since only the rich could afford the expense of buying and maintaining these wigs the term 'big wig' came to be applied to men of wealth and importance.

seventeenth century they kept their natural hair. Women's formal hunting dress, though, did include a wig. In the eighteenth century women's hairstyles became more flamboyant and from the 1760s false hair was used but combined with the natural hair. The high styles of the 1770s and the wide ones of the 1780s needed considerable padding and so elaborate were they that frequently they were not taken down for several weeks.

WIGMAKING TOOLS

The tools of the wigmaker altered little over two hundred years. Hackles, with long metal prongs set obliquely into a wooden base, were used to disentangle the hair and pairs of drawing brushes with either bristles or metal pins were used to straighten and sort the hair.

Pipeclay hair curlers survive in large numbers. They were made from the seventeenth century to the early nineteenth. Early ones are often hand-shaped and sometimes hollow, but from the second half of the eighteenth century they are more uniform and occasionally they have the initials of the maker on the end. Boxwood, cane and willow ones were produced from the late eighteenth century and had the advantage that they did not get so hot.

Hair intended for wigs was given a permanent curl by winding it round the curler, boiling it in water and then heating it in an oven. It was not uncommon to take the hair to the bakery, where it would be wrapped in brown paper, enclosed in a protective pastry crust and then put in the oven.

A hair loom was used to make lengths of hair fringe from the treated hair. Two upright weaving sticks were clamped to the bench, three silk threads stretched between them and small quantities of hair knotted by the root ends on to the thread. The knots were pushed up tightly

RIGHT: *A bag wig of about 1780 with black satin bow and two bags that belonged to Sir Thomas Worsley of Platt Hall, Manchester.*

BELOW: *Madame Pfob's was a wigmaking business in the Royal Arcade, Norwich, which closed in the 1970s. The two weaving sticks in the foreground fitted into the wooden clamps and were used for weaving hair weft. Behind are two pairs of nineteenth-century pinching irons and a heavier pressing iron for setting curls. The spiked object is a heckle for combing out the hair and the wooden block had the foundation net fixed to it while a wig was made.*

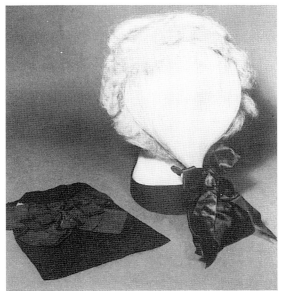

A barber's shop in 1772. The customer has hung his bob wig over the back of the chair. A number of different wigs are on stands and hang from the wall and it was not unusual for a barber to stock twenty or thirty different styles. Notice the barber wears an apron and appears to be lathering his customer with a cloth or sponge.

together and a length of hair fringe made. The fringe could then be used for making hairpieces or sewn spirally on to the foundation net of a wig. The other way of making a wig is to knot the hairs individually on to the foundation net. In either case a wigmaker's block is needed to act as a base. This was made from solid wood or shaped hollow leather.

Maintaining a wig, especially a seventeenth-century one, was a difficult task best left to the professional. Greasy wigs had to be treated with spirits rather than washed as water loosened the hairs. Curls were reformed, protected by a triangle of folded paper called a papillote, and then pressed with heated pinching irons. These iron scissor-like tools had solid spoon-shaped ends in the eighteenth century, and flattened circular ends at a later date.

POWDERING AND THE POWDER TAX

The powdering of wigs began about 1715. Lighter wigs were in fashion and at first they had been bleached but the hair soon became faded and discoloured so people started to use powder made from finely ground starch or wheat flour scented with orange flower, lavender or orris root and occasionally coloured blue, violet, pink or yellow.

The wig was first greased with pomade made from hog's grease, tallow or a mixture of beef marrow and oil. Then one of a variety of powdering devices was used. There were tiny pairs of bellows, wooden powdering carrots, so called because of their shape, pumps made from wood and leather, and powder puffs made from swansdown or silk threads.

The fashion for wigs was dying in the late eighteenth century and finally expired following the introduction of a tax on powder in 1795 by a government needing to finance the wars against revolutionary France. Those wishing to continue powdering had to have a powdering certificate, for which the fee was 1 guinea per year, although concessions were made for fathers with more than two unmarried daughters. The wig soon went out of fashion and the tax, which yielded over £200,000 in its first year, was gradually less successful until it

ABOVE: *A powdering cloth, two powdering devices, a collection of pipeclay hair curlers and a wig stand (centre) and two wig stands or millinery stands. The powdering cloth is of hand-blocked Indian cotton, about 1730. It fitted round the neck to protect the clothes while the wig was powdered. The small wood and leather bellows are of a design first used in the eighteenth century and continuing in use into the twentieth century in the theatre.*

BELOW: *An eighteenth-century wood and leather wig powderer. It was filled with powder and flicked or pumped back and forth.*

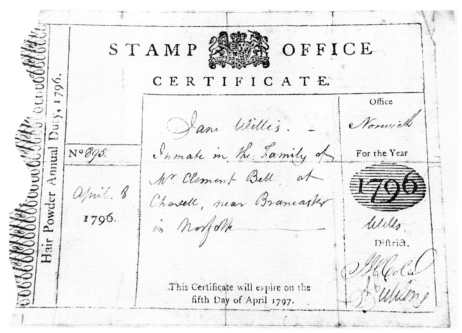

A hair powder duty certificate for 1796. This cost a guinea and speeded the decline of powdering and wigs themselves.

was repealed in 1869, when only liveried coachmen and footmen still wore powder.

FALSE HAIR

From the early nineteenth century men no longer wore wigs overtly although 'invisible coverings' were available to disguise baldness. Their crude construction was improved in 1867 when a fine hair lace of human hair was developed for wig foundations in America.

For women, however, hairpieces or 'transformations' were widely advertised and used, and it was estimated in 1863 that wigmakers were using 100,000 pounds (45,000 kg) of hair a year. Bonnet curls were added at the sides of the face, chignons could be pinned on and individual puffs and curls were pinned in to improve on nature.

In the 1920s false hair went out of use with the fashion for the short hairstyles known as the bob and the shingle, except for those who wanted, on formal occasions, to look as though they had retained their long hair.

In the 1960s there was a revival of interest in wigs with the cheap 'fun wigs' made from Asian hair or acrylic. They were machine-made in Hong Kong, where by 1969 there were over three hundred factories mass-producing them, so that 13 per cent of all women in Britain owned a wig.

ABOVE: *Nineteenth-century 'transformations'. False hair was frequently used to augment nature. (Top row) Pin curls, plaits, hair for a chignon. (Below) Bonnet curls, which were tied in place with ribbon at the back of the neck. The junction and ribbons would have been hidden by the bonnet and the face beneath the brim flattered by the luxuriant curls.*

RIGHT: *A fun wig of the 1960s in Jean Shrimpton style, machine-made from Asian hair. Wigs like this were cheap and gave instant length.*

Eadie's barber's shop, Glasgow, about 1900-10. The striped pole was the traditional trade sign going back at least to the middle of the eighteenth century. The dark aprons worn by the barbers were also traditional but much deplored by those in the smarter end of the trade who had moved on to white jackets by then.

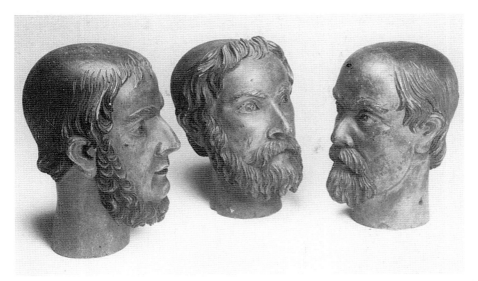

Barbers' blocks. These carved and painted wooden heads were probably used by a barber to illustrate the hair and beard styles available about 1850-60.

SHAVING EQUIPMENT

In 1540 the barbers' trade guild was amalgamated with that of the surgeons and until the two trades separated again in 1745 the range of services offered was far wider than hair cutting and shaving. Barber-surgeons were able to practise blood letting, treat wounds and lance abscesses.

The barber's pole is a reminder of this original work. In the late eighteenth century barbers had a blue and white striped pole and surgeons the same with a red flag and blood pot attached. Later the barber's pole was variously blue and white, red and white or red, blue and white, and the red is said to represent blood from the blood letting, and the white the bandages. Alternative trade signs were a large metal shaving bowl or in some cases a carved and gilded wooden bear (from the popular bear's grease hair dressing).

Barber's bowls are mistakenly referred to as bleeding bowls. They are shallow with a broad rim and made from earthenware, porcelain, metal or wood. The customer generally held the bowl to his neck, the U-shaped indentation in the rim fitting round it, and the barber used the bowl to catch lather and whiskers.

In the seventeenth and eighteenth centuries soap balls were hand-shaped or moulded and stamped with the maker's name, and pierced spherical silver soap boxes were available for domestic use. The barber might alternatively use powdered soap perfumed with orris root. In the nineteenth century shaving soap came in pottery jars with transfer-printed lids and later liquids, sticks and creams were available. The firm of Pears advertised widely, claiming their shilling stick would last twelve months.

Shaving mugs were used by barbers and in the home and came into production about 1840. They had a compartment for soap and one for water and were often heavy in the base to avoid spillage. Frequently made by continental factories, they were often decorated with scenes of British resorts and were bought as souvenirs. They are being reproduced today.

It is said that shaving brushes were

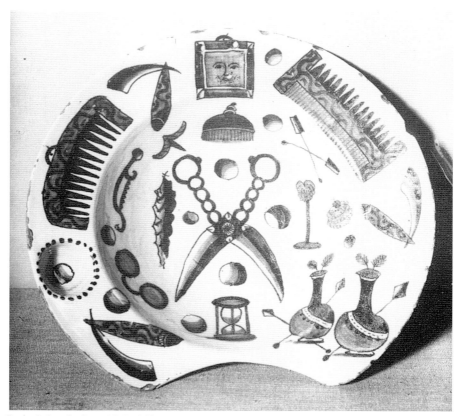

Barber's bowl, about 1740, delftware. These bowls are sometimes referred to as bleeding bowls but their principal purpose was to catch water and lather during shaving. The indented rim fitted round the customer's neck with a depression for the soap. The bowl illustrates many of the barber's tools.

introduced from France in the 1750s but their use was not universal until a century later. Before their introduction barbers used a sponge or their finger tips to create a lather. Badger hair was popular for its softness and long life but hog's bristle was cheaper and often favoured by barbers. Handles were made from bone and metal and from boxwood, whose fine grain does not easily absorb water.

RAZORS

Samuel Pepys used pumice to smooth his beard before he developed the courage and skill to shave himself with an open razor. At first he shaved once a week and then daily but this was unusual and until the twentieth century most men chose to be shaved once or twice a week by a barber.

Early razors seldom survive except from excavations. Late eighteenth-century razors have straight handles which are often made from horn and sometimes decorated with large rivet washers or inlay. The blades are wide at the 'point', tapering to the handle end, and there is no shoulder to separate the blade from the tang. The blades are triangular in section.

After 1800 a shoulder appears and from about 1815 file cuts along the tang and blade back stop the finger slipping. Hollow grinding was introduced in the early part of the nineteenth century to aid honing and gradually became more pro-

RIGHT: *Silver shaving jug, 1713, of oval baluster shape with sparrow beak spout. It would have been filled with hot water in the kitchen by a servant. The handle is insulated with leather binding.*

BELOW: *Shaving equipment. Shaving sticks made by Yardley, Fields, Palm & Olive (in infringement of the Palmolive trade name), Gerard, Gibbs, Dubois and Colgate, tins of Vinolia and Oowana shaving soap and a Vinolia pot lid. The open razor in the foreground is a cardboard replica advertising Pears shaving soap. Other items include a plated shaving stand, about 1932, a shaving mug of continental porcelain, three bristle shaving brushes, one of which is imitating badger, an Ever-Ready razor and three packets of razor blades.*

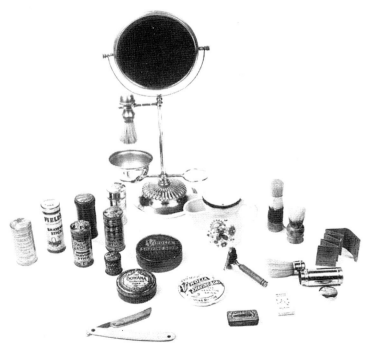

ABOVE: *Price list of William Addis and Son, about 1890. Badger hair was more expensive than hog bristle and was used for the higher quality shaving brushes. 'Hat', 'Broom', 'Standard' and 'Turnback' are handle designs.*

Unusual mid nineteenth-century picture of a barber's shop in Drygate, Glasgow, showing the simple equipment needed: open razor, shaving brush and soap, hairbrush, tonic bottle and on the wall a strop, mirror and advertising plaque for bear's grease.

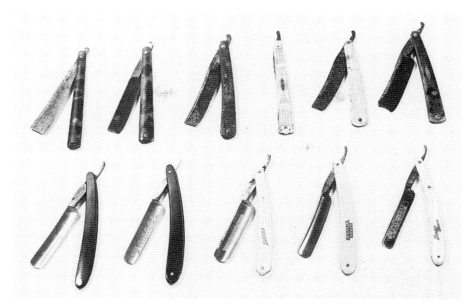

Open razors. Top row, left to right (all handles are horn stained as tortoiseshell except where stated): straight handle, triangular section blade with little division between blade and tang, about 1800; separation of blade from tang, marked 'Marsden Warranted', about 1815; pressed horn scales with inlaid brass decoration, about 1840; ivory handle with silver piqué decoration, about 1840; bone handle, about 1840; heavy blade marked 'Johnson Silver Steel', about 1830. Bottom row (all handles plastic and all blades hollow ground): Wilkinson, marked 'Tuesday' on back of blade, from a seven-day set, late nineteenth/early twentieth century; Golta, English silver steel and English ground, twentieth century; Timor razor made in Solingen; Bismarck razor, early twentieth century; Dovo-Inox razor, German, 1950s.

nounced. Various improvements in the quality of steel are charted on razors. 'Cast Steel' or 'Acer Fondue' occur after 1770 until the 1830s, 'Silver Steel' from about 1820 and 'Indian Steel' from about 1840. Another guide to dating is that from the 1820s the sovereign's initials were sometimes stamped on the blade.

Horn handles in the first half of the nineteenth century were often pressed with elaborate sporting, classical or commemorative scenes. There are few tortoiseshell handles but many horn ones stained to look like tortoiseshell. Wood was used occasionally but the best quality ones were ivory and mother-of-pearl. In the 1840s piqué decoration with tiny silver pins driven into ivory was common.

Celluloid was discovered in 1868 and some of the various black plastic handles are difficult to distinguish from horn. Imitation ivory, developed in 1870, is more easily distinguished by its unnaturally straight and even graining. Hollow grinding became extreme in the 1870s and 1880s when machine grinding became possible and much of the work, even on Sheffield blades, was done in the German steel town of Solingen. Many of the blades were etched and gold washed.

Guards were put on open razors in the eighteenth and early nineteenth century but the first real development in the design of a safety razor came with Monk's L-shaped frame in 1874. The frame held a single-edged blade and acted as a guard as well. The Star safety razor was the first hoe-shaped razor. Patented by the Kampfe brothers in 1876 in America and 1887 in Britain, it was widely marketed.

Seven-day set of open razors, in red leather case, by Walker and Hall of Sheffield, early twentieth century. Sets marked with different days of the week on each blade were available from the 1820s.

The blade was like a short section from an open razor and it was provided with a holder so that it could be used on a conventional strop.

In 1895 King Camp Gillette designed a razor with a wafer-thin steel blade, sharp on both sides, clamped between guards with the handle fixed in the centre of the blade. Production started in 1903 and soon the product was enormously successful.

Gillette blades had green wrappers until the eve of the Second World War and from 1906 the name and portrait of Gillette was used as a trademark. The diamond trademark was introduced in 1908. In 1929, to prevent competitors' blades from fitting Gillette razors, a blade design with three holes and a long slot in the centre was devised and in the 1930s some new cheap lines were introduced to combat competition; the Gillette Blue Blade came out in 1932 and the Thin Blade in 1938.

There were hundreds of other firms in the market, especially after 1921, when Gillette's patent ran out. Some produced single-edged blades, others double-edged designs, and several, such as the Auto-Strop Company, devised designs for stropping blades without removing them from their handles.

The next important development was the stainless steel blade, which Wilkinson Sword sold in 1956 and improved in 1961 by giving it a silicon coating. Gillette had been in the market briefly from 1928 to 1932 with their orange-wrapped Kroman, but without much success, and they only belatedly re-entered the field in 1963. These coated stainless blades dominated the market until the new bonded systems were introduced in the 1970s.

Many tools and gadgets began to be powered by electricity in the 1890s but although a patent for an electric razor was taken out in 1900 in the United States, there was little serious manufac-

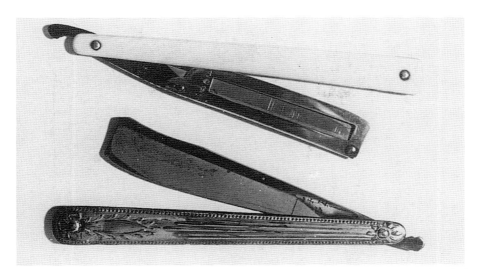

ABOVE: *Open razors. (Top) An ivory-handled steel blade with removable silver guard, hallmarked 1801, said to have been used for shaving George III after he went mad. (Bottom) An unusual old Sheffield plate handle, blade by George Brittain, late eighteenth century.*

BELOW: *A collection of safety razors. (Left to right) Rolls Razor, single-edged blade with stropping and honing surfaces inside container, 1940s; Ever-Ready single-edged razor in tin, 1950s; razor patented 1912; Monk's design frame razor, patented 1875, with single-edged blade, manufactured by Watts, about 1900, with handle for stropping single-edged blade; Darwin Universal Hollow Ground Razor, with stropping and honing surfaces inside container, 1950s; Valet Autostrop razor with strop in Bakelite box, 1940s, design patented 1904; 7 O'Clock razor for double-edged blade and with comb guard in Bakelite case, 1950s; Gillette razor with comb guard; Ever-Ready shaving cream, 1951; Ever-Ready razor and single-edged blades in plastic holder, 1951; Myatt razor with comb guard, 1950s.*

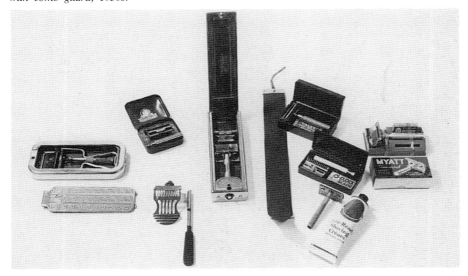

Safety razor blade packets. In the third row from the right are three Gillette packets and the bottom one is the green packet used from 1906 until just before the Second World War. The Blue Blade was introduced in 1932 and sparked off a host of imitations in blue packets. The Ace of Blades (bottom right-hand corner) was made in the 1920s by G. T. Money of South Creake, Norfolk. Made entirely by British labour, it claimed inside 'Britannia rules the Shaves'. Some of the packets illustrate the different designs for the holes in the blades. The trick was to design blades that fitted everyone else's razors but razors that fitted only your blades.

ture of them. The first successful dry shaver design was developed by Joseph Schick, a retired American army colonel. Patented in 1928, it was on the market in 1931 and, like the early Remington model of 1934, was based on oscillating clippers. Philishave developed its rotary-headed model in 1937 but it was not available in Britain until 1947. Another early manufacturer was the Glasgow Sunbeam factory, whose design was adapted by Braun. Other areas of experiment were mechanically operated versions with systems of gears to work the cutters; there were clockwork razors and in 1951 Philishave brought out its first battery-operated version.

HONES AND STROPS

Hones were used to sharpen open razors by grinding the metal down slightly and giving the edge a new set of teeth. Belgian, German or slatestone hones were all made from natural rocks and lubricated with either oil, water or lather. Pike's hone, the swaty hone and carborundum on the other hand were all synthetic compositions. Carborundum, a compound of carbon and silicon, could be quite coarse and was more useful for rubbing down razors with notches or gaps than in producing a fine shaving edge.

Strops did not grind the edge. In use the teeth on a blade (visible only under a microscope) bend backwards. The use of a strop realigned them. There were two main categories of strop. The hanging strop had a strip of leather, preferably horsehide, on one side and canvas on the other, a hook at the top and a handle at the base. Six strokes first on the canvas then on the leather before and after shaving kept the blade in good condition. The alternative design was a hard rigid

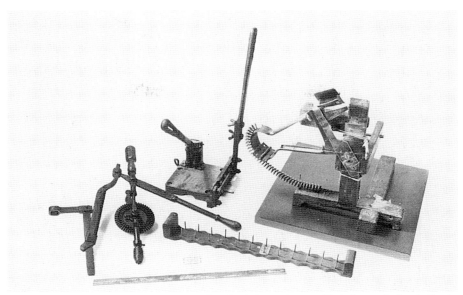

ABOVE: *Equipment said to have been used in G. T. Money's razor blade factory in South Creake, Norfolk, in the 1920s. He bought coils of metal strip from Sheffield and developed his own method of sharpening and tempering. He claimed to be the first person to produce razor blades in strips rather than cut the steel to length first. Gillette did not move to this method until 1930.*

BELOW: *Some early electric razors were designed like an ordinary safety razor but had an electrically powered oscillating blade. This German design was patented in Britain in 1932.*

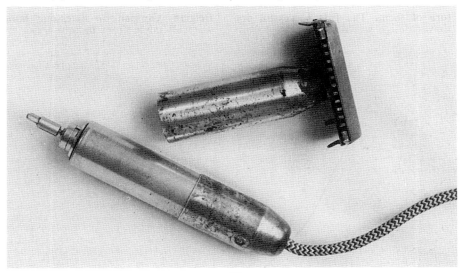

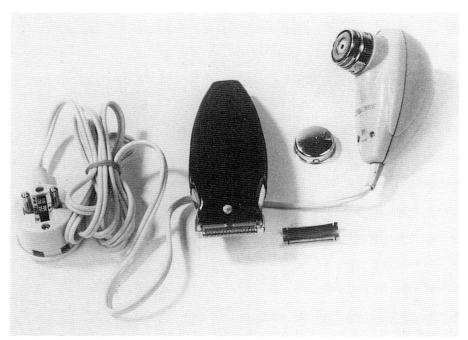

ABOVE: *Two early electric razors. (Left) The Rolls Razor Viceroy Dryshaver, 1940s. There was also a mechanical version of this. (Right) Philishave's rotary model marketed from 1948 to 1954. Many early models came with current adaptors.*

BELOW: *A collection of strops and hones. (Front left) The Ross Vienna Tri-sided Strop; (centre) wall hanging strop; (right) strop made from a cabbage stalk. Lillicrap's hone, in green glass, was patented in 1930 at a period when glass hones for safety razors were in fashion. To the right of it is a Belgian hone, the thin yellow side being the part used for sharpening open razors.*

strop up to 12 inches (305 mm) long with a handle. Generally these strops had two surfaces but some had three or even four and many of the designs were patented.

As soon as Gillette brought out his safety blades devices were invented to strop them. Despite constant exhortation on the packets to throw away the blades after use these machines proliferated and since people already expected to strop an open razor it was natural for them to do the same to a safety razor blade.

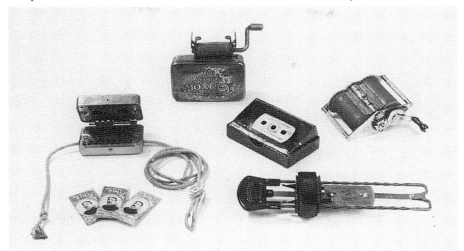

ABOVE: *Many ingenious devices were patented for sharpening Gillette-type safety razor blades despite the manufacturers' insistence that blades be thrown away after use. (Left to right) A device in a brass box; when the cord is pulled the spindles turn eccentrically, rubbing the blade across the Bakelite projections; patented 1933. Kirbee Monkey Strop, costing 2s 6d and claimed to give two hundred shaves from every blade; patented 1919. Simple glass strop, about the 1930s. Sharpex, with two wheels running on twisted rods, about the 1920s. Be-Be strop, German design, patented 1922.*

BELOW: *Moustache cups. Early in Victoria's reign moustaches were curiosities worn only by foreigners, but from about 1850 they first became fashionable, then respectable. About 1855 Harvey Adams and Company, the Staffordshire potters, started to produce these cups with little pierced shelves near the top on one side to protect the moustache whilst drinking. They were popular for the next fifty years. Many were German imports and they were frequently sold as gifts or souvenirs.*

The reconstruction of a barber's shop in the Museum of London. Notice the 'Singeing' sign and the hot towel urn. The use of hot towels spread from America, where A. Shultz, working as a hairdresser in a Boston hotel in 1878, first used them to help clients with skin problems. After a shave he steamed their faces with a very hot towel, gave them a finger massage and followed this with further towels. By the 1930s the hot towel urn was quite common.

Hairdressings, clippers and scissors. The brilliantine tins include Fields, Lustressa, Vinolia, Boot's Tonair and Pears. The bay rum was supplied by Hovenden and Sons, hairdressers' sundriesmen, in 1925 and still has its original seal. There was a 6d deposit on the returnable bottle.

HAIRDRESSING

TRIMMING THE HAIR

Only in the late nineteenth century did hairdressers' scissors become specialised, with open shanks and long narrow finely tapered blades. Fringe scissors were produced with one blade serrated so that the hair did not slip. Clippers were an American invention. From the mid nineteenth century many designs were patented but these were principally two-handed versions for trimming horses. It is said that in the early 1870s some American youths used some to give each other 'pineapple' haircuts, the predecessor of the crewcut, and Brown and Sharpe, manufacturers of clippers, took out the first patent in 1879 for hair clippers. Adjustable versions were developed and early in the twentieth century electrically powered ones were made.

Singeing was introduced early in the twentieth century. It was supposed to strengthen the hair, stop it splitting and prevent it from 'bleeding' after a cut. A wax taper or later an electrical device was passed across the ends of the hair and the charred ends were removed by vigorous rubbing.

HAIR DRESSINGS

Pomade was mentioned in Gerard's *Herbal* of 1597 and continued to be made into the twentieth century. The original ingredients were pig's lard and apples but various animal and vegetable bases were used later, scented with flower oils.

Parallel with the sale of pomade went the sale of specific greases. Once wigs were abandoned men looked for something to promote hair growth and suggest masculinity. Bear's grease fulfilled this function. Bears were readily available in Russia and the Alps and their meat was still eaten in Europe. Bear's grease was first used in Paris and soon after in London. It was sold in small ceramic pots which by the 1830s had pictures of bears on the lids. Atkinsons continued to manufacture bear's grease until the early twentieth century but the market was overtaken by oils and greases of non-animal origin.

ABOVE: *In the nineteenth century hairdressings were supplied in pottery containers with transfer-decorated lids. This lid for a pot of bear's grease was made by the Pratt factory, between 1845 and 1860.*
LEFT: *This rare advertising plaque for Rowland's Macassar Oil, about 1860, shows that it was intended for women as well as men. Antimacassars were specifically designed to protect chair backs from this sticky hairdressing.*

Macassar oil came from the seeds of an Indian oak tree. The yellowish-white oil used since the early nineteenth century gave rise to that fussy bit of Victorian furnishing, the antimacassar.

The fashion for bay rum started in the United States in the nineteenth century and rapidly spread to Europe. The genuine article came from a crude alcohol obtained during the manufacture of West Indian rum and which was then distilled with fresh leaves and berries. It was believed to stimulate hair growth but was also used as a face rinse after a shave.

Brilliantine comes in two forms, solid and liquid. The base is either vegetable or mineral oil. The stiffer variety is thickened with waxes and the liquid variety is thinned with spirit. It is often perfumed with flower oils, Yardley first manufacturing their lavender brilliantine in 1920.

Hair tonics, dyes and restorers have always been popular but many have contained poisons like lead or irritants like spirits of rosemary or acetic acid. Henna was the safest dye used before the introduction of aniline dyes in the 1920s. Harlene and Koko were two tonics widely advertised in the Edwardian period and Koko was even said to invigorate the brain.

HAIRBRUSHES

Brushes have been commonly used for hairdressing only since the late eighteenth century. High quality hairbrushes were made from hog's bristle, which came principally from Russian wild boar until the famine of 1920-1 disrupted supplies and importers turned instead to China. Today India is a major source.

Occasionally vegetable fibre was mixed in to cheapen the brushes. It originally arrived in Britain as a packing material.

There was a patent for whalebone bristle in 1808. It was cut with compound guarded knives and used for extra hard brushes. India-rubber was patented in 1853 and in 1888 the Birmingham firm of Hinde patented a wire hairbrush. Nylon was first marketed in 1938 and was soon adapted for brushes.

The backs of high quality brushes were made from ivory which came from West Africa and India. The stock or back of the brush was drilled with holes at regular intervals. For wire-drawn brushes the holes went right through. Women

ABOVE: *Two chrome-finished hairdresser's tonic dispensers and a black glass and aluminium Brylcreem dispenser. Brylcreem was produced by the County Chemical Company, Birmingham, in 1928 and originally it was sold only to hairdressers.*
BELOW: *Bristle picking and sorting for Addis Limited in the 1920s in Hertford. Sorting for colour and quality is still done by hand.*

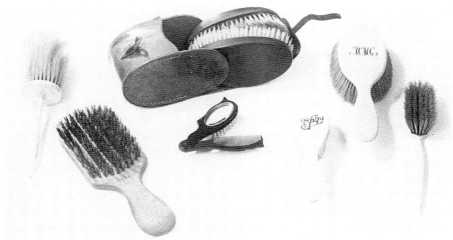

ABOVE: *Brushes. (Left to right) Neck brush, ivory and hog's bristle, late nineteenth century; hairdresser's brush with wooden slotted back, made by Britton's, whalebone and hog's bristle, 1950s; pair of military hairbrushes with ebony backs in leather case, 1950s; moustache brush, comb and mirror set, buffalo horn with hog's bristle, sold for up to 1s 9d in Harrod's in 1895; baby's brush, celluloid on wood back, soft bristles, about 1915; hairbrush from set, ivory and hog's bristle, early twentieth century; hairbrush, bone or ivory back, stiff hog's bristle, nineteenth century.*

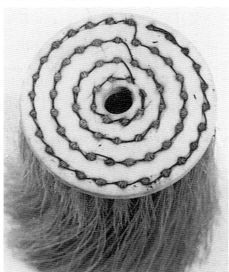

LEFT: *Interior of ivory and bristle neck brush showing the method of wire-drawing a brush. Holes were drilled in the back, tufts of bristle pulled through and fixed in place by a continuous length of wire.*

clamped the stock to the workbench and using a thin flexible brass wire or a strong thread drew knots or tufts of bristles into each hole in turn using a continuous length of wire. When each hole was filled the wire was secured and a back put on the brush. A skilled worker could draw five hundred knots an hour.

For higher quality trepanned brushes the holes did not go right through the back. Long holes were drilled from end to end through the brush back to form tunnels connecting the rows of knot holes. A waxed thread was doubled and passed through a long hole and pulled up as a loop using a hook in the extreme end hole. A tuft was drawn into the hole and the thread was then pulled up through the next hole. This process was repeated until each hole in the row was filled, when the long hole was plugged with ivory and the thread cut.

By the 1880s wire drawing was in decline. Filling machines had been developed and patent brushes, such as the Mason Pearson brush of 1885 with bristles set in a rubber pad, required other methods.

Barbers' rotary hairbrushes were first patented by Edwin Camp of Bristol in 1862 and they remained in general use until after the First World War, continuing into the 1970s in some traditional shops. The large brushes were each fitted with a large pulley wheel which engaged with a continuous belt hanging from a turning shaft above each chair. The barber held the handles and pressed the brush on to the customer's head. Many patents were registered including hand-cranked and clockwork ones and in 1904 the first with an integral electric motor.

COMBS

Combs were a necessary part of the hairdresser's equipment long before brushes. Early combs were made from boxwood, bone, ivory, tortoiseshell and in particular horn. Horn was imported from Russia, South America and South Africa as well as Europe and was removed from its core, steamed, flattened and polished. The teeth were cut individually with a double-bladed hand saw called a stadda which cut a small notch to position the next tooth at the same time. Then they were filed with wedge-shaped files called floats and polished. In the nineteenth century machines were invented for speeding the process, using a circular saw to make several combs at once or by cutting from above.

The advent of plastic in the late 1860s made combs much cheaper. At first they continued to be hand-cut from plastic sheets but soon they could be moulded by machine. The British Xylonite Company produced celluloid combs with the trade name Ivoride or Xylonite. Vulcanite could also be used but horn continued in use for singeing as it does not burn easily. Artificial tortoiseshell was possible and by introducing metallic pigments iridescent effects could be produced.

HAIRDRESSERS AND THE HAIRDRESSERS' GUILD

There was a huge growth in the hair-

Combs. (Clockwise from the centre back) Derbac comb for removing nits, 1940s; double-ended bone comb, hand-cut; horn comb cut diagonally across the grain; black hand-finished plastic comb; comb moulded from Xylonite, a brand name for celluloid; comb moulded from Lactoid, a brand name for casein, an early plastic made from milk solids, early twentieth century; baby's comb with very fine teeth moulded from Xylonite; double-sided plastic baby's comb with painted decoration in imitation ivory; tortoiseshell comb in mother-of-pearl case, late eighteenth century; moulded moustache comb with hinged case; black plastic comb with case and pearlised decoration, 1930s; brass comb with bone case, early nineteenth century.

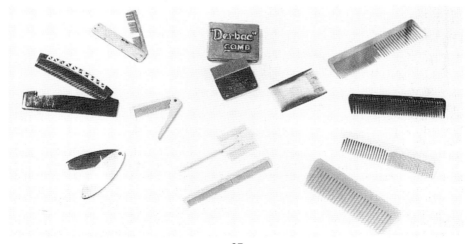

dressing trade in the second half of the nineteenth century, out of all proportion to the growth of the population. It was becoming increasingly fashionable to have one's hair attended to outside the house and women especially provided a new market. Whiteley's store in Westbourne Grove, London, opened the first hairdresser's shop in a department store in 1876 and ladies' hairdressing became a lucrative trade.

The term 'hairdresser' was not, however, applied exclusively to the female trade. As business expanded a number of prominent hairdressers sought to establish high standards. In 1882 they founded the Hairdressers' Guild, which united wigmakers, hairdressers, perfumers and kindred trades 'to improve the social position of the trade'. H. P. Truefitt, head of the oldest established hairdressing firm, became master and they set about creating new hair fashions and held evening classes to raise standards. In this they were behind the French for in the 1760s Legros de Rumigny had opened the first hairdressing academy, with courses for hairdressers, valets and chambermaids.

HAIR TONGS

Curling irons were used in the sixteenth century and the design remained the same until well into the nineteenth century. The scissor-like device with two rounded prongs was heated and then clamped and twisted in the hair. Curling irons were indistinguishable from laundry goffering irons and, if necessary, it was even possible to improvise with a fork or use a flat iron on plaited hair. By 1765 a new design was in use. One of the prongs was grooved and the other fitted into this groove. This became the standard design in the nineteenth century and sometimes the handles were sprung.

Variations included box crimping irons with two corrugated blocks of iron which fitted into each other in place of the prongs. Crimping irons had two or four prongs on one side and three to five on the other. When closed the prongs passed each other.

Curling irons could be heated on the fire or the range or a special stove could be used, fired by charcoal, methylated spirits or tablets, gas or from 1894 electricity. Internal heating with iron rods was another variation.

A collection of comb cleaning devices. When natural materials were used for combs many could not stand scouring in hot water so various cleaning devices were developed. The comb was run along the cotton comb strop, on the right. The long horsehair of the two other devices was dragged through the teeth of the comb.

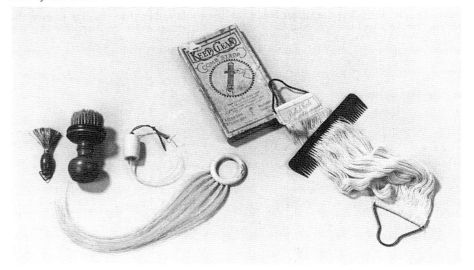

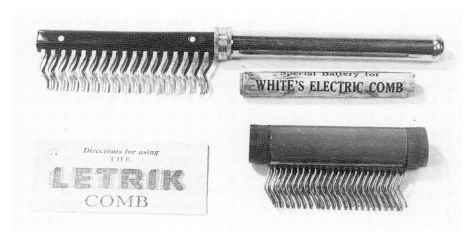

From time to time there were vogues for electric hair combs. White's Comb was patented in 1927. The battery was permanently connected to the teeth of the comb but the connection between the two sets of teeth was only made by running it through the hair. The electricity was said to stimulate hair growth. The Lectric Comb worked on the same principle.

In the late nineteenth century the use of hair tongs was revolutionised by Marcel Grateau, a French hairdresser. In 1872 he developed a new technique of waving by placing the groove under the hair and moving the hair backwards and forwards to produce a natural S-shaped wave. People, including the singer Nellie Melba, flocked to his salon and he was able to retire in 1897, aged forty-five. He published his methods and started to market special tongs made only by Maison Pelleray. The tongs had the same prong and groove as previous ones but were loose fitting. There were irons of four sizes from A to D and the prongs were larger in diameter than previously. Many cheap copies were made.

PERMANENT WAVING

To make a permanent curl in hair it needs to be boiled or steamed or baked. The first person to develop a method for doing this reasonably safely on growing hair was Charles Nessler, a London hairdresser. His method was first publicly offered in 1906 and consisted of borax pads and an electric heater. In his first year he had only eighteen customers but this was hardly surprising since his method was very expensive, was not infallible and took up to twelve hours. By 1922 it was commonly used in America and followed in Britain two years later.

M. Eugene tried to perfect the method by placing the heating element nearest the roots rather than the tips to give the hair a more even curl and by using a special sachet that oiled the hair and kept it from drying out. Subsequently various other systems were developed.

The home perm arrived in the 1930s. It relied on chemical pads that needed no machines to generate the heat to set the curls. Several versions were available but they frequently smelt bad and could take up to eight hours. One of the most successful was Toni, which came out in 1944.

HAIRPINS AND CURLERS

In the eighteenth century hairpins were generally straight but by the nineteenth century they were bent back on themselves. Numerous different styles of undulation were tried to find a pin that would not work loose. The trade centred on Birmingham, where in 1911 there

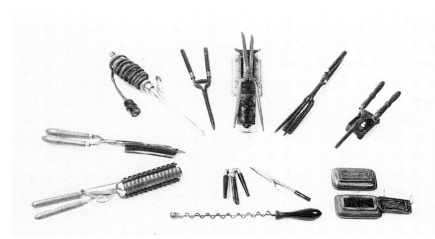

ABOVE: *Hair tongs. (Foreground) George Lichtenfeld's Automatic Waver and Curler, patented 1891. (Behind) A pair of folding travelling curling irons and a pair of Rola tongs, about the 1920s. (From the left, clockwise) Harlene Home Hair Waver, price 2s 6d, about the 1920s; tongs, early twentieth century; electric waving tongs, Bakelite plug for light socket, 1920s; sprung handle curling tongs; Marcel waving tongs on heater which can either be fuelled with liquid methylated spirits or solid fuel blocks, 1930s; four-pronged (originally five) crimping iron, nineteenth century; small curling tongs on heater, nineteenth century; two 'La Favorite' curling tong heaters, twentieth century.*

BELOW: *A collection of hairpins and curlers. (Top left) Early heated hair curlers patented in 1891 but still in production in the 1920s. Below them, a curl stick around which curls were formed then slipped off and pinned in place, early twentieth century. (Bottom) Leather-covered curlers, early twentieth century, and a variety of patented curlers from the 1890s to the 1960s. (Centre right) Plastic brush rollers which came in with the looser styles of the 1950s.*

were about fifteen manufacturers, one of the largest being Kirby, Beard and Company. When the new very short hairstyles, the bob and the shingle, became fashionable hairpin sales slumped. So the firm developed the first spring pin, registered in 1924, which they called the Kirbygrip.

In the late nineteenth century much effort went into designing hair curlers. Hindes of Birmingham patented many pivoted ones and in 1891 came the precursor of the heated roller, a hinged curler with a heated rod that fitted down the central tube. The brush roller arrived in the 1950s and the large plastic jumbo rollers came with the bouffant styles of the early 1960s.

HAIRWASHING

It would have been thought odd to wash one's hair with water in the seventeenth century. The usual method was to comb powder through the hair but this frequently made the problem worse.

The term 'shampoo' is a Hindi word for massage and it was first used in England in the eighteenth century. By the mid nineteenth century it started to be applied to washing the hair with soap and water and this method of cleansing the hair became thought of throughout Europe as the English method. In France in the 1890s several Englishmen were employed by fashionable hairdressers especially to shampoo customers. The more normal method there and in some English shops was to use spirits but this went out of fashion after several deaths from inhaling the fumes.

Shampooing taps with mixed hot and cold water were used in the nineteenth century and later back-wash basins were produced. Sachets of shampoo generally held soap powder until after the Second World War. Following the development of detergents in the 1930s the first soapless shampoo, Drene, was marketed in the USA in 1933.

HAIRDRYERS

Drying long Victorian hair was a problem. Brushes with hollow teeth were invented which could be filled with hot water and some would take a heated metal bar but a more sophisticated

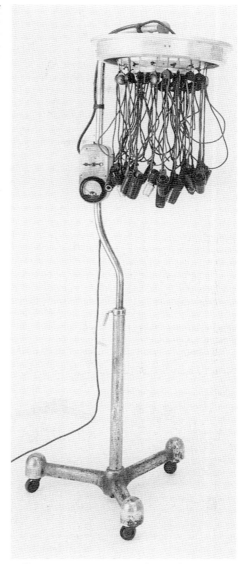

Icall permanent waving machine, about 1930.

solution was needed by professional hairdressers. In the 1880s and 1890s several gas dryers were patented and Beyer's patent of 1893 was manufactured. These early dryers had a stand and came with a hood attachment which allowed the customer to be left. They relied on convection, an electric fan not being fitted until 1900. The trumpet-shaped design was patented by H. Halliwell in 1903 with a gas burner and electric fan. In 1905 the first portable version was produced with an electric fan and an optional electric heater.

To some extent hairdressing has gone full circle in the last three hundred years. Men can again take an interest in their appearance, natural henna and curling tongs are back and wigs are bought in large numbers.

PLACES TO VISIT

Below are some of the many museums with social history collections that display wig, hairdressing and shaving bygones.

UNITED KINGDOM
Museum of Nottingham Life at Brewhouse Yard, Castle Boulevard, Nottingham NG7 1FB.
  Telephone: 0115 915 3600. Website: www.nottinghamcity.gov.uk
Museum of London, 150 London Wall, London EC2Y 5HN.
  Telephone: 020 7001 9844. Website: www.museumoflondon.org.uk
People's Palace and Winter Gardens, Glasgow Green, Glasgow G40 1AT.
  Telephone: 0141 276 0788. Website: www.glasgowmuseums.com
Sheffield City Museum, Weston Park, Sheffield S10 2TP.
  Telephone: 0114 278 2600. Website: www.museums-sheffield.org.uk

UNITED STATES
Colonial Williamsburg, Williamsburg, Virginia 23185. Reconstruction of a wigmaker's
  shop and wigmaking demonstrations. Website: www.history.org
Shelburne Museum, Shelburne, Vermont 05482. Very large collection of open razors.
  Website: www.shelburnemuseum.org

FURTHER READING

Adams, Russell B. *King C. Gillette: The Man and His Wonderful Shaving Device*. Little,
  Brown and Company, Boston, 1978.
Ball, A. *The Price Guide to Pot-Lids and Other Underglaze Multicolour Prints on Ware*.
  Antique Collectors Club, second edition 1981.
Cooper, Wendy. *Hair: Sex, Society and Symbolism*. Stein and Day, New York, 1971.
Cox, James Stevens. *Dictionary of Hairdressing and Wigmaking*. Hairdressers
  Technical Council, 1966.
Doyle, Robert A. *Straight Razor Collecting*. Collector Books, Kentucky, 1980.
Foan, Gilbert A. (editor). *The Art and Craft of Hairdressing*. The New Era Publishing
  Company, c 1933.
Woodforde, John. *The Strange Story of False Hair*. Routledge and Kegan Paul, 1971.

COLLECTING

Anyone wishing to make a collection of hairdressing equipment should have no difficulty. Many items find their way to junk stalls and jumble sales and the dressing table drawer may well provide the nucleus of a collection. There are few specialist dealers although some concentrate on razors. Neil Wayne, Old Chapel, Bridge Street, Belper, Derby, specialises in high quality shaving items.